ANIMAL FA

Goril

NOEL SIM

illustrated by

J. M. Dent &

London   To

Commended by IUCN (International Union for Conservation of Nature and Natural Resources)

First published 1978
Reprinted 1979
Text © Noel Simon 1978
Illustrations © J. M. Dent & Sons Ltd 1978
Reproduced and printed in Denmark by Grafodan Offset
for J. M. Dent & Sons Limited
Aldine House, Welbeck Street, London
This book is set in 14 on 16pt Imprint 101
ISBN 0 460 06761 3

Contents

Introducing the Gorilla

Of all the primates—the order of mammals which includes the monkeys, apes, and ourselves—none is more likely to impress us than the gorilla. It is without question one of the most imposing animals in the world.

In describing the gorilla it is difficult to avoid comparing him with man. For the gorilla is in many ways very human to look at. Not only does he belong to the same family as ourselves, he is also our closest relative. But his size and strength are much more striking than ours. An adult male gorilla is as tall as a man. But it is not so much the animal's height as his girth that is astonishing. No man that ever lived had such a broad chest, so massive a head, such huge hands or long arms. It is not unusual for an adult male's arm-spread to be 8–9 feet (about 2.5m). His legs, on the other hand, are short and comparatively weak. And, of course, he has no tail.

You would imagine that an animal as large as the gorilla could hardly have escaped notice and would therefore have been known to man for a long time. But it is only a short while—hardly more than a century—since the gorilla was first discovered. Even then its habits remained little known until Dr George Schaller carried out the first detailed field study of wild gorillas. From 1959 he spent a year living with them in the forest. It was through him that we at last gained a clear idea of how gorillas live and began to understand the true character of these splendid animals. Many of the beliefs about gorillas, which until then had been accepted as true, were found to be wrong.

The first people to see gorillas in the wild assumed them to be terrifying monsters, hideous and savage beyond words. The gorilla looks so nearly human that it is easy to see how this mistake arose. Such huge, shaggy, near-human creatures lurking in the depths of the forest—itself a rather frightening place for those who are not used to it—must surely belong to a race of giants or demons. And as they were obviously enormously powerful—far stronger than any man—it was taken for granted that they must behave as people assumed a giant would behave, using their colossal strength for sinister purposes. Before long stories began to spread that the gorilla was extremely ferocious. And, as stories often will, they improved with the telling. Hunters, catching a glimpse of an adult male gorilla in the depths of the forest roaring and beating its chest, were so certain that they were about to be attacked that they did not hesitate to shoot

8

in 'self-defence'. So, largely through our own ignorance, the gorilla acquired an evil reputation which it did not deserve.

Thanks to the work of Dr Schaller, and others who followed him, we now know better. Although the gorilla is certainly gigantic, he is a gentle giant. For all his size and tremendous strength he is quiet and easy going, wanting only to be left alone to live his life in peace.

Where the Gorilla Lives

The gorilla is found only in Africa, and not outside the Zaire River Basin—the country through which the Zaire River and its tributaries flow. Within this general region there are two main areas in which the gorilla lives. The larger of the two is in West Africa, stretching from the northern bank of the Zaire River to southern Nigeria and inland to the Ubangui River. This is where the lowland gorilla lives. The second, and smaller, area lies farther inland, in the highlands of eastern Zaire, reaching from Lake Edward to the western side of Lake Tanganyika. It also extends across the floor of the Eastern Rift Valley to a point where the borders of Uganda, Rwanda and Zaire meet. This is the home of the mountain gorilla. A gap several hundred miles wide separates the two areas.

The two types of gorillas—the lowland and the mountain—have been separated from each other for a very long time. Because the mountain gorilla lives in a cooler climate than the lowland gorilla, it has a more shaggy coat. Its coat is also blacker.

It would be wrong to imagine that gorillas live everywhere

9

within these two areas. They are widely scattered in small groups. Parts are unsuitable for them. They also seem to avoid many of the places which would appear to suit them.

Habitat

One of the reasons why the gorilla remained unknown until such a short time ago was because of the nature of its habitat—the type of country in which it lives. For the gorilla is an animal of the tropical rain forest.

Rain forest is very dense. Inside the forest it is difficult to see more than a short distance. Many of the trees are huge. Some of them are higher than a ten-storey building. But it is not so much these tall trees which limit the view as the thick layer of undergrowth at ground level which stands more than head high. In such surroundings even an animal as large as the gorilla is difficult to see.

Occasionally the undergrowth thins out. There are also clearings—more or less open patches—where the vegetation is not so thick. A gorilla in a clearing would be visible, but if he is in heavy undergrowth an occasional glimpse of an arm or a hand is all that would be seen. Sometimes the only sign that he is there is the vegetation swaying as he moves. And, of course, he usually is in the undergrowth, because that is where he finds his food.

What is more, the gorilla's eyesight is far sharper than man's. He will generally be the first to spot any movement. Gorillas miss very little that happens in the forest.

Growing Up

Gorillas have no particular breeding season. Adult females reproduce about once in four years, giving birth to only a single young. The baby is born after a gestation period—the time taken for it to develop inside its mother—that is only a few days shorter than for human babies. It is born with a light skin. This slowly becomes darker. By the age of two months it is very dark, almost black. At birth it has almost no hair except for a little on top of its head, its back, and the outer surface of its limbs. Otherwise it is naked. But it soon acquires a covering of soft baby hair which it keeps until the age of about three months. Then it is replaced by adult hair.

For the first two months of its life the baby gorilla is helpless and completely dependent upon its mother for everything it needs. She suckles it when it is hungry, cradling it in her arms. While the group is on the move or feeding she carries it. At night she sleeps with it in her nest. All the time she watches and cares for it, comforting it if it is hurt, and grooming it to keep it clean and healthy. When it rains, the mother uses her body to shield her baby from the rain. Even when the group is resting, the infant is never far from her side or reach.

While the baby is small it does not have the strength to cling to its mother's fur. The baby gorilla's ability to cling is very feeble—less developed, in fact, than in any other large primate. The mother must therefore hold it all the time, except when the group is resting. Usually she holds it with one arm against her chest. As the baby's strength increases it becomes better able to grip. Gradually it grows strong enough to hold on without its mother's help. When nearly four months old it works its way around to its mother's back and rides between her shoulders, hanging on to her hair for support.

For the first few months of its life the infant feeds entirely on its mother's milk. At two to three months it starts to develop rapidly. It experiments with eating leaves and other vegetation. By the time it is about seven to eight months old it lives almost entirely on plant food. Weaning normally takes place by the eighth month, though some youngsters may continue to suckle occasionally—if their mothers allow—for as much as another year.

Six-month old gorillas are already showing the first signs of loosening their ties with their mothers. They are then beginning to crawl on their own. And their mother is encouraging them to

do so. By the time the infant is about one year old its mother no longer minds allowing it out of her sight. She carries her infant until it is about one year old. Soon after, and certainly by the time it is eighteen months old, she gives up carrying it altogether.

The ties between mother and baby, which in early life are so close, become weaker after the age of about one year. From that time on the young gorilla becomes less dependent on its mother and more and more linked with the group. This is particularly true of the young males. The mother-daughter bond is stronger. Seldom is it entirely broken. It often continues—though naturally in a less intensive form—even after the youngster has become completely independent of its parent. This usually occurs at the age of about three years.

Other members of the group are kind and considerate to the youngsters. This applies not only to the females, who are naturally interested in babies other than their own, but to the adult males as well. Silverbacked males often allow youngsters to take liberties which would be almost unthinkable if they came from an older animal.

Gorillas take a long time to grow up. By the age of about six years the female is fully grown. Until then, males and females look very much alike. But after the female has stopped growing the male continues to put on weight and muscle for a further two or three years until he is nine or ten years of age. By then he is much bigger and more massively built than the female. The shape of his head also changes. The skull of the adult male rises to a prominent crown, or crest, on top of his head. This crown is used to 'anchor' the large muscles required to work the gorilla's jaw, for powerful jaws and strong teeth are needed to chew the

tough vegetation on which the gorilla feeds. These muscles are attached to a bony ridge on top of the skull. Females do not have this crown, or at least not nearly such a prominent one.

At the same time, a patch of silvery-gray hair begins to appear on the male's back. This grows into the shape of a saddle. By the age of twelve years the saddle is fully formed. The combination of larger size, dome-shaped head, and saddleback makes it easy to identify the adult males, and to have a very good idea of their age. The older the animal the grayer he becomes. With increasing age the gray hairs spread over more and more of his body, except for the arms which always remain black. Adult females also become somewhat gray with age, but their gray hairs grow only on certain parts of the head, neck and shoulders.

16

Social Life

Gorillas live in family groups. A group may contain up to as many as thirty animals. Usually, though, groups are less than half that size. Each group includes one or more adult silver-backed males, several blackbacked—younger—males and females with their young of various ages. A typical group might include one silverback, two blackbacks, half a dozen females and their young.

A group wandering through the forest meets other groups from time to time. The probability is that most of the groups in a particular area are known to each other. Meetings between groups are normally peaceful. On rare occasions a serious fight takes place between adult males during which one or other may be bitten so severely that he dies. But this hardly ever happens. Normally the males are content to make their protest by peaceful means. They may rant and rage and make a great deal of fuss and noise, but usually they stop short of actual violence.

A gorilla's attachment to its own group is very strong. There is seldom any attempt to leave it for another. When two groups meet they may stay together for a time, the females and young-sters mixing together briefly, if only out of curiosity and the wish to be sociable. But, after a while, when their curiosity has been satisfied, they drift apart to continue feeding.

Although these close-knit groups form the basis of gorilla society, there are in addition a number of adult males living on their own. These lone males sometimes come to join a family group. They may stay for as little as a few hours or as long as several months, but eventually they tire of being with the group and wander away to resume their lonely existence.

It sometimes happens that a female will go along with a lone male when he leaves. This is one of the ways in which a new group is founded. A new group may also form when a group becomes too large and splits up. One of the adult males and several females may spend less and less time with the main body until eventually, almost without realizing it, they leave it altogether and start living on their own.

A group spends its life in a fairly small area, getting to know every part of it. But, unlike many other animals, the gorilla does not have a territory for its own use. Other groups use it as well. The various groups live peacefully together. They have little reason to fall out with one another. Food is plentiful and easy to find. There is more than enough for all. And as gorillas are neither bad-tempered by nature nor easily jealous, there is little cause to fight among themselves.

The Leader

A gorilla group is always led by an adult male, a silverback. It is he who decides when the group shall feed, rest, or move, and which way it shall go. He shows that he is ready to move by standing in a special way with his legs and arms spread more widely than usual and held rather stiffly. Sometimes he keeps this pose while strutting—that is, walking stiffly—a short distance. In this way he makes quite clear to the others in the group

18

that the time has come to move. But although the leader decides these matters, this does not mean that he is always at the front of the group. Sometimes he is in the middle and sometimes at the rear.

Every member of the group—male as well as female—has to obey the leader and have respect for his wishes. Each male knows his own rank and gives way to his superiors. But this applies only to the males. Among the females the situation is different. The females, of course, give way to the leader and the other adult males. But among the females themselves there is little sign of rank. All females are more or less equal though, if anything, those with young babies may be treated with greater respect than those without.

The leader is not always the eldest silverback in the group. What is more, change of leadership does not involve a desperate battle between rival silverbacks. When an old male is past his prime he is not thrown out of the group, as happens with many animals. He simply stands down in favour of the next most suitable candidate. He is then allowed to remain with the group, but in a less exalted position which he is content to accept.

Food

Most of the gorilla's time is spent either sleeping or eating. Gorillas eat nothing but plant food, most of it obtained from the scrubby undergrowth on the forest floor. Very little of their food comes from the trees.

A great part of their diet consists of the leaves and juicy stems of a variety of shrubs, vines and other plants, such as wild celery and ferns. It also includes fruits—the wild fig, for example— when in season, as well as berries, flowers, and pieces of bark. Gorillas also like certain roots, which they dig out of the ground. Like many other animals, gorillas are very fond of the tasty white bamboo shoots which sprout during the rainy season. When they appear the gorillas may move into the bamboo forest for days at a stretch. They either break the shoots off at ground level or pull them out from beneath the surface. Wild honey also attracts them. But to get it they have to raid the nest and rob the combs in the face of furious attacks by angry bees. Their habit of eating thistles and nettles must be almost as uncomfortable, for both the African bee and the African nettle have much more vicious stings than those with which we are familiar.

With some plants gorillas peel off the outer skin, dropping it on the ground and eating only the juicy pith. Or they may gnaw out the pith with their teeth. Sometimes they raid cultivated land in search of growing crops, particularly maize, sugarcane and bananas. Oddly enough, though, it is not the fruit of the banana which attracts them but the pith in the trunk of the tree itself. To get at this delicacy, they tear down the entire tree. Naturally enough, this does not make them very popular with the farmers.

Despite living in the tropics, gorillas seem never to drink in the wild state. This is because the vegetation on which they feed is so juicy that it gives them all the liquid they need.

When feeding, the gorilla likes to stand with the weight of his body taken on his feet and one arm, leaving the other hand free for plucking vegetation and feeding. But plant food is so plentiful in the rain forest that he is frequently able to obtain all the food he wants just by sitting in one spot. He then uses both hands, one after the other, to pluck any leaves, stalks or flowers within reach that take his fancy. If particularly hungry, he uses one hand to cram food into his mouth while the other is busy collecting the next mouthful. Certain plants which are long or stringy are rolled into a ball before being stuffed into his mouth. When all food within reach has been eaten, the gorilla moves a few steps, again squats, and repeats the process.

In this way the group moves so slowly that even though animals may not be able to see one another in the thick undergrowth they are unlikely to lose touch. It is easy to see where gorillas have been feeding, for their trail is marked not only by their footprints but by the litter of torn vegetation which they scatter on the ground as they go.

Movement

If a particularly delicious item of food catches their eye, gorillas may sometimes reach it by standing erect on their legs, leaving both hands free for collecting and eating. They may even move a few paces in an upright position. But they do not walk more than a very short distance in this way. Except for one or two unsteady steps, they rarely walk upright unless there are branches or bushes which they can hold with their hands for support.

Their normal method of moving over the ground is on all fours, supporting themselves on the knuckles of their hands. They lean on their knuckles because their arms are so much longer than their legs, though most of their weight is carried on their hind legs with the soles of their feet flat upon the ground. When moving slowly gorillas walk straight ahead, but if in a hurry they move slightly sideways.

When moving through the forest from one place to another, the silverbacked male will usually lead, a blackbacked male will be at the end of the column, and the females will be strung out in a straggling line between them. But if, as more frequently happens, the group is merely feeding there is no particular order. Each animal potters about wherever suits it best.

Tree Climbing

The gorilla is one of the small number of primates—man is another—which has moved down from the trees to live on the ground. Although the gorilla is capable of climbing trees, his great size and weight naturally place a limit on his ability as a climber.

Gorillas climb trees for a variety of reasons—either in their search for special items of food, perhaps to see better, or simply to rest or sleep. The branch of a tree is often drier than the damp ground. You might think that they climb as protection against possible enemies. But that is unlikely. If alarmed, gorillas at once make for the ground—a sure sign that they feel safer on the ground than in the trees. Except when they are sleeping, gorillas spend almost all their time on the ground.

When climbing trees, gorillas have to be careful how they do it. Often they test the strength of a branch or creeper, to make sure it can support them, by giving it a sharp tug before putting their weight on it. If, as sometimes happens, a branch were to break, they could crash to the ground and be hurt.

To climb, the gorilla pulls himself up with his powerful arms. His feet are used mainly to carry the weight of his body. If there are no branches close to the ground which he can hold, the gorilla simply reaches around either side of the tree with his long arms and heaves himself up by sliding his hands up the trunk, at the same time pushing with his feet.

Some primates have feet that can be used almost like hands, and big toes that are rather like thumbs. They can therefore use their feet for holding on to branches. But the gorilla's feet are more like our feet. They cannot grasp. The gorilla therefore has to be careful to hold branches tightly with his hands. Most monkeys find it easy to move rapidly through the trees, leaping nimbly from branch to branch, or jumping from one tree to another. But for an ape the size of the gorilla this is out of the question.

Coming down a tree, the gorilla descends feet first. If the branch on which he is sitting is not far from the ground he may lower himself, hanging by his hands and swinging for a few moments as though trying to decide where to land, before dropping on to his feet. If there are no branches close to the ground, he will slither backwards down the tree in much the same way that he climbed it, using his feet as brakes and with his arms clasping either side of the trunk.

Tree climbing is naturally easier for young gorillas than for adults. The older and heavier they become, the more they are likely to avoid climbing trees. Gorillas feel much happier on the ground. The old males, in particular, seldom leave it.

26

Nesting

The gorilla's last activity of the day is to build a nest in which to spend the night. Each day at dusk, shortly before dark, the leader suddenly stops collecting food and starts to make a nest. This is the signal for the others to follow.

You probably think that only birds build nests, and may find it difficult to believe that an animal as large as the gorilla should also build a nest. You may have even more difficulty in believing that the gorilla makes a new nest every day of its life. But, strange as it may seem, all the great apes—the chimpanzees and orang-utan as well as the gorilla—build nests. So do the more primitive primates—the lemurs, lorises and tarsiers. But, with one possible exception, their relatives the monkeys do not.

When a bird builds a nest it must make it strong enough to last an entire season—long enough to hatch its eggs and raise its brood. A bird's nest must therefore be carefully made. This takes time, trouble and care. But a gorilla's nest is altogether different from a bird's. It is meant to be used no more than once. Then it is abandoned. The next night the gorilla will be somewhere else and will build another. Even if he is not far from where he slept the night before, he will still build a new nest rather than go back to the old. Old nests are not used again, though they remain visible for months.

If suitable trees are at hand, the gorilla likes to build his nest in them, for he prefers to sleep above the ground. But if the trees are too frail to bear his weight the gorilla will nest on the ground. As the females are lighter than the males, they find it easier to

nest in the trees—either on a stout branch or wedged in the fork
of a tree. But the adult males have more difficulty. Their greater
weight generally forces them to nest on the ground. Often they
sleep at the foot of a tree. If the trees are unsuitable the females,
too, will nest on the ground.

Sometimes nests may be high up in the trees. But usually they
are not far from the ground. Members of a group do not always
nest close together. Often they are quite widely separated. Each
gorilla chooses its own site and builds without regard to other
members of the group. It would seem reasonable to think that
the building of a nest suitable for an animal as large as the gorilla
would be very complicated and take a long time. Surprisingly,

though, it seldom takes more than a few minutes. Having chosen the site, the gorilla simply stands, squats or sits in the centre, reaches out with his arms and pulls towards him any small branches and boughs within reach. Some he holds in place with his feet. As the stems or branches are drawn in, he bends them without breaking them off and thrusts them around and under himself, tucking in twigs and leaves until he has made a rough platform.

During the season, when bamboo shoots are sprouting, gorillas may remain for days at a time in the bamboo forest. They then build their nests in the tops of the bamboo, which grows in clumps like gigantic blades of grass. The bent tips of the bamboo canes, when drawn together, form a comfortable platform which sways gently with every breath of wind.

The reason why a gorilla builds a nest is, of course, simply to keep himself from falling out of the tree or, if on the ground, from rolling away in his sleep. But ground nests are built even when the ground is level and they appear to serve no useful purpose. They are usually of even simpler construction than tree nests. Often they are very crude indeed. Ground nests seem to be built more out of habit than for any other reason, as they are of little practical use. This habit is so strong that gorillas often build nests even during the midday rest period.

Even quite young gorillas have an instinctive urge to build nests. Long before they leave their mother's nest they experiment with nest building. While waiting for his mother to build her nest, a young gorilla may move a short distance away and quickly build a nest of his own before returning to his mother for the night.

Each gorilla builds his own nest. The only exceptions are young gorillas which use their mothers' nest. Not until they are almost three years old do young gorillas sleep on their own. They may then, for a while, share a nest with another infant. Adult gorillas never nest together.

When in the nest the gorilla may lie either on his back or on his tummy with arms and legs tucked in close to his body for warmth. A mother with a small baby sleeps on her side with her legs curled up and an arm around her young, cuddling it close to her chest for warmth and protection.

The Day's Routine

Getting up in the morning is a much more relaxed business than going to bed. And it is carried out much less eagerly. No doubt the nest is every bit as difficult for the gorilla to leave as bed is for us. The process takes place slowly, according to the mood of the individual.

The appearance of the first light of dawn is a signal for the gorillas to start stirring in their nests. An arm thrown over the side of a nest and quickly withdrawn shows that they are beginning to wake up. One or two sit up and gaze about in a slightly dazed manner. They survey the scene through half-shut eyes and without much enthusiasm. After a bout of stretching, yawning and scratching they may lie down again to snatch a few more minutes in bed, for bed, whether it be a spring mattress or a tree, is never more comfortable than at the moment of leaving it. A

hand reaches out of the nest to grab a nearby branch and pull it towards a hidden mouth. The owner of the hand plucks and chews the leaves slowly as though in a dream. But the urge to eat gradually becomes stronger than the urge to stay in bed. The leader is first to be up and about. The sight of him feeding shames others into joining him. But it may be an hour or more before every member of the group is on the ground and feeding.

By the time the last animal has left his nest the other members of the group are already spread out through the undergrowth feeding as they go. The latecomers hurry to join them, and soon make up for lost time. The group feeds without a break for several hours. By the middle of the morning the gorillas have eaten so much that they can take no more. They are glad to pause for their midday rest.

The midday siesta is a time for the adults to rest and the youngsters to play. The adults lie around in every imaginable attitude. Some sprawl on their backs, their legs and arms flung out at all angles. Others sit with their backs propped against tree trunks, arms cradling their over-stretched tummies. As they slowly recover from the effects of their meal, some of the adults occupy themslves with social grooming. A few groom themselves, but most prefer to have another do it for them. An animal wishing to be groomed will 'present' itself to a companion—a request which is seldom refused. It carefully combs through the other's coat, using one hand to part the hair, and the fingers of the other hand—often helped by the teeth—to remove burrs, thorns, ticks, dirt, flakes of dried skin, or anything else which should not be there. Mothers take special care to groom their infants from the earliest age. Baby gorillas are very demanding. They need constant attention, much as human babies do. A female either holds her baby in one arm, leaving the other free for grooming, or she lays it across her lap. However hard the infant squeals and squirms, the mother pays no attention.

In this way the gorilla keeps its coat spotlessly clean. But there is much more to grooming than keeping clean. The close contact and touch which are an essential part of grooming are as important as cleanliness. This personal attention allows the animals to relax, to reduce tension. From the contented looks on their faces it is clear that gorillas enormously enjoy being groomed. They like it so much that they go almost into a trance —as people sometimes do when having their hair brushed.

While the babies remain by their mothers, the older youngsters play. Among the young gorillas' most popular games is 'follow-

my-leader'. They move in a line, one behind the other, clambering into a huge fallen tree, crawling along its spreading branches, and jumping off the end on to the ground, then sliding on their bottoms down a slope.

The game then switches to 'hide-and-seek' among the bushes. They trail in and out among the dozing adults, circling around a clump of nettles and scrambling over a log. Becoming bored with that, they race wildly about, wrestling and romping with one another, or leaping into the air to swing from a low-lying branch. One youngster hurls himself at a hanging vine, using it like a trapeze to swing backwards and forwards. Another rushes off waving his arms like a berserk traffic cop before rolling head over heels and collapsing in a heap with a self-satisfied smirk on his face. One more daring—or more foolhardy—than the others attempts to climb up the mountainous side of the silverbacked male. Instead of being angry, the leader takes it all good-naturedly. Even when the cheeky youngster celebrates reaching the summit by tweeking the hair on his head the big male does not seem to mind.

If it rains the scene is very different. Gorillas hate getting wet. And in the rain forest where they live it rains frequently at certain seasons. Mothers with small babies hold them close in an attempt to keep them warm and dry. But for the adults there is little escape. They huddle at the foot of a large tree or beneath an overhanging branch, seeking whatever protection they can. Any females or young animals lucky enough to find a dry spot are not likely to keep it for long. An adult male has no hesitation in pushing them out and taking their place. The rain deluges down, pouring off their thick coats. No doubt they are as miserable and dejected as they look. But before long the rain lets up, and the gorillas are able to resume their interrupted routine.

By early afternoon hunger is again causing the group to become restless. The silverbacked male, as always, is first to move. As soon as he starts feeding the females at once follow. Mothers with small babies gather them into their arms as they go. The older offspring, still busily playing, are ignored. Their mothers move off on their own, leaving the youngsters to catch up as best they can. This, of course, brings indignant cries from the youngsters. Thinking themselves abandoned, they race after their mothers, grabbing any fur within reach, and hauling themselves up like passengers boarding a moving vehicle. They climb straight into their accustomed place between their mothers' shoulder blades.

The afternoon passes in much the same way as the morning, for gorillas need to eat a large quantity of plant food to satisfy

their appetites. The group wanders slowly through the under-growth, fully occupied with feeding, until dusk once again calls a halt to its activities.

Chest Beating

As they move slowly through the forest, the gorillas remain constantly alert for possible danger. The crack of a breaking branch or the unexpected appearance of a strange animal will cause the leader to give a sharp grunt of warning. This alerts the other members of the group. They stop feeding, move closer to him and anxiously follow the direction of his gaze.

If the strange animal appears to be a threat, the leader will sound a warning roar which thunders through the stillness of the trees. The power—the sheer volume—of the silverback's roar is enough to scare even the bravest animal. The sudden explosion of sound bursting upon the silence of the forest is ear-shattering. If the stranger does not take the hint and go, the leader may thump his own chest like a drum. No other animal expresses itself in this way. All gorillas, even young ones, beat their chests, but the silverbacked males give by far the most impressive performance.

The silverback does not start to beat his chest all at once. He builds up to a climax by a series of other actions. First, he usually hoots. He starts fairly calmly, but gradually works himself into a state of excitement. The other members of the group, knowing what is about to happen, stand back a few paces to give him plenty of room. His hoots become louder and more frequent until they gradually merge into an almost unbroken flood of sound, ending in an ear-splitting screaming roar. He becomes very put out if another member of the group interrupts him. If that happens, he pauses and starts again at the beginning. He emphasizes his feelings by grabbing leaves and holding them in his lips or thrusting them into his mouth. Sometimes he bites at twigs or branches, or simply pulls and shakes them violently. As his excitement mounts, he picks up soil, tears off branches or uproots small bushes and hurls them into the air. The climax comes when he suddenly stands upright and, raising himself to his full height, beats his chest with the cupped palms of his hands. This gives off a hollow sound which carries a long distance. Sometimes he uses only one hand. He may also beat other parts of his body, or indeed a tree or anything else that happens to be handy. In the meantime the other gorillas gather behind him, peering at the cause of the trouble and perhaps joining in by beating their own chests. At times the group may hide in the surrounding undergrowth, leaving their leader to demonstrate on his own. That done, he may, while still standing erect, run a few steps forwards waving his arms and tearing at the vegetation as he goes, before dropping on to all fours. He finishes by slapping the ground with the palm of his hand.

However alarming this may be to a human observer—particularly to anyone who does not know what to expect or what it is all about—this seemingly terrifying performance is largely bluff. It is in fact a sign of nervousness. The whole of the gorilla's elaborate display is a means of releasing tension, a safety-valve for blowing off steam—just as we ourselves sometimes need to do. Like us, the gorilla feels much calmer when the outburst is over. Chest-beating can occur even when there is no cause for anger or defiance, simply as a means of expressing the sheer joy of living.

As often as not these 'scenes' take place when a strange male appears unexpectedly close to the group. When this happens the silverbacked male may follow up his display of chest-beating by advancing a few steps towards the stranger, growling, jerking his head and gnashing his teeth. If this does not bother the stranger, the leader may take a further step or two, waving his arms wildly in the air and making a series of quick passes at him. If, even then, the stranger does not retreat, the leader may finally charge. He moves fast on all fours, often screaming with rage as he goes. But a charge generally stops short of actual bodily contact. The leader then thrusts his face forward until it nearly touches the other's and glares at the stranger. There is something almost unreal in seeing two such immensely powerful animals standing practically nose to nose and staring each other out. But even among people an unbroken stare makes your opponent feel nervous and unsure of himself. After glaring for a while one of the males will suddenly turn his back on the other and stalk away.

If the stranger decides to submit, he does so either by shaking his head or by crouching down and lowering his head and presenting his back to the leader. This shows that he intends no harm and accepts the other as his superior.

Gorillas show other moods and feelings by a series of facial expressions and gestures which bear an uncanny resemblance to those used by humans. Sadness, anxiety, pleasure, anger, frustration, and fear are emotions which affect the gorilla as they do us. The gorilla responds to them much as we do ourselves. As animals cannot talk, their looks and gestures have to take the place of speech, and therefore have much more meaning to an animal than to a human being.

Facial expressions are usually accompanied by sounds which help to make their meaning even more clear. These range from the gentle burbling purr of contentment to the full-throated roar which signifies anger. Between these two extremes are a variety of squeaks, chuckles, barks, grunts, hoots, screams and yells.

While the leader is quick to respond to any possible threat from an outsider, he is remarkably good-natured with members of his own group. It is not often that he has to exert his authority. When he does so he is treated with respect and obeyed at once.

From time to time squabbles naturally flare up between members of the group, but serious fighting hardly ever occurs. Most of the quarrels takes place among the females. They scream

42

and yell, slap and push, bare their teeth, and pull each other's hair. Usually the silverbacked male ignores them. He does not bother even to turn his head to look. But if their squabbling goes too far, with fur starting to fly, he may prevent the situation from getting out of hand by moving towards them and grunting sharply. Their quarrels instantly stop.

There is very little friction between the adult males of the group. This is partly because there is hardly any jealousy over females, but mainly because every male knows and accepts his place in the social order. This is extremely important in avoiding fighting which might harm the group. Perhaps the reason why female gorillas quarrel so much more than the males is because they do not have any regular rank in the social order. The fact that they are all supposedly 'equal' leads to endless bickering.

Enemies

The only large predator—flesh-eating animal—to share the rain forest with the gorilla is the leopard. While young gorillas—now and again even adults—are taken, the leopard usually hunts smaller prey.

Gorilla numbers are kept down not by predators but by various diseases and parasites. This is particularly true of young gorillas. It is unlikely that more than about half the gorillas which are born survive to become fully grown.

Apart from disease, the main killer of gorillas is man. Local tribesmen are very fond of gorilla meat. But although gorillas are killed by hunters, the main threat to their survival is not so much from hunting as from destruction of the forest in which they live. As the number of people increases, more and more land is needed for planting food. The local people therefore want the land for themselves, either for growing crops or to provide more grassland for their cattle, sheep and goats.

A limited amount of temporary clearing and cultivation is not harmful to the gorilla. It may even benefit them. For when farmers abandon their plots—which they normally do after a few years—the forest gradually returns. The new growth contains a great deal of the gorilla's favourite plant food. This secondary forest is in fact the type of habitat that the gorilla likes best. But when agriculture becomes permanent, a very different situation arises. The land is then never allowed to revert back to natural forest. As the human population increases, more and more of the natural forest vanishes, leaving less and less room for the gorilla.

Conserving the Gorilla

In theory it should be an easy matter to conserve the gorilla. The gorilla does not wander over vast distances like the elephant. It does not kill domestic animals like the lion. Nor is it dangerous to man. All it needs is a suitable area of unspoilt rain forest in which it can be free to follow its own way of life. As long as it is not disturbed, a gorilla family group does not need a very large area in which to live. But it cannot live where it is being constantly harassed or disturbed.

Several national parks and game reserves have already been set aside in various parts of the gorilla's range, and in most of the countries in which it occurs the gorilla is protected by law. But the law is not always enforced, and the sanctuaries are not always well cared for.

If the gorilla is to survive it is essential that these national parks and game reserves should become sanctuaries in truth and not merely in name. In the vastness of equatorial Africa it should not be too difficult to find room for the gorilla—if only man cared to do so.